BIBLE BRAINTEASERS

BIBLE
BRAINTEASERS

Bob Phillips

HARVEST HOUSE PUBLISHERS
Eugene, Oregon 97402

Bob Phillips is the executive director of Hume Lake Camps, one of America's largest youth camping programs. Bob is a licensed marriage, family, and child counselor and the author of over 20 books including the popular *Encyclopedia of Good Clean Jokes* and *Ultimate Bible Trivia Challenge* with more than two million copies in print.

BIBLE BRAINTEASERS
Formerly titled: *Bible Fun*
Copyright © 1987 by Harvest House Publishers
Eugene, Oregon 97402

Library of Congress Catalog Card Number 87-081034
ISBN 1-56507-119-0

Printed in the United States of America.

Introduction

I n our fast-paced society we often do not take time to have fun. Sometimes we even feel guilty when we take a moment to relax. When was the last time you slowed down and got your mind off the pressures of a busy life? When was the last time you treated yourself to a mini-vacation?

BIBLE FUN is designed to provide many hours of satisfying entertainment, growth, and learning. It will give you bite-sized escapes to refresh your mind and spirit. You'll get a big kick out of coming up with solutions to the:

- Word Hunts
- Versigrams
- Tail Tags
- Patch Word Puzzles
- Anagrams
- Bible Riddles
- Impossible Mazes
- and much more

You can sharpen your skills, test your Bible knowledge, and challenge your mind all at the same time. You may like to use some of the puzzles with your family as a mealtime diversion or as a method of learning while traveling by car. Some of the games and riddles lend themselves to a group challenge at a Bible study or Sunday school class. You may want to share BIBLE FUN with a shut-in or someone who's in the hospital. How about sending a copy to a missionary friend as a change of pace.

Some of the puzzles are easy and some more difficult. It wouldn't be fun if they were too easy. So just jump right into whatever catches your fancy. Have a great time. If you get stuck, the answers are in the back of the book. You can peek if you want to — no one will be watching.

We hope you won't struggle too much. Just enough to experience the joy of learning and the satisfaction of solving a problem through your own resourcefulness. If you like these puzzles and have some of your own ingenious variations that you think others would enjoy, drop us a note and include them.* Your suggestions and encouragement may spark MORE BIBLE FUN.

> Bob Phillips
> Hume, California

*Bible puzzles, riddles and games — along with clean jokes can be mailed to:

> P.O. Box 9363
> Fresno, CA 93792

Beatitudes

See how many of the Beatitudes from Matthew 5:3-11 you can identify.

1. Blessed are the _____ : for theirs is the kingdom of heaven.

2. Blessed are they that _____ : for they shall be comforted.

3. Blessed are the _____ : for they shall inherit the earth.

4. Blessed are they which do _____ : for they shall be filled.

5. Blessed are the _____ : for they shall obtain_____.

6. Blessed are the _____ : for they shall see God.

7. Blessed are the _____ : for they shall be called the children of God.

8. Blessed are they which _____ : for theirs is the kingdom of heaven.

9. Blessed are ye when men shall _____ you and _____you, and shall say _____ , against you _____, for my sake.

Odd
or Even

To discover this important Bible event cross out the letters above all the odd numbers.

J	O	B	E	R	A	S	T	M
18	11	3	4	17	39	36	7	51

U	E	U	S	E	A	W	P	E
10	29	13	42	1	9	8	47	16

W	E	P	O	T	T	E	R	Y
19	73	84	55	41	30	33	21	15

Forbidden Fruit Maze

How did Eve get to the forbidden fruit?

START

Something the Israelites Faced

In eight moves can you go to letters that spell something the children of Israel faced in the wilderness?

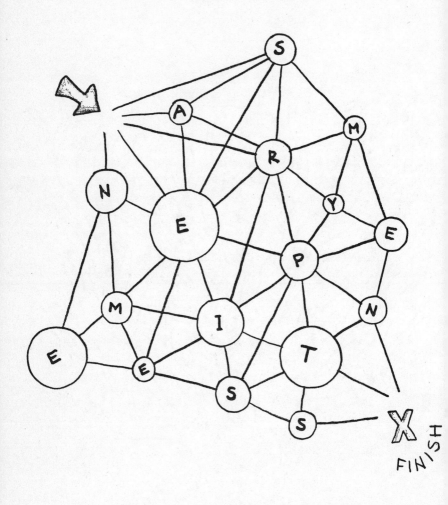

Things Missing
In Heaven

In the book of Revelation the apostle John lists
a number of things that will not be in heaven.
How many of these can you remember?

1. _____
2. _____
3. _____
4. _____
5. _____
6. _____
7. _____
8. _____
9. _____
10. _____
11. _____
12. _____
13. _____
14. _____
15. _____
16. _____
17. _____
18. _____

Bible Labyrinth

Hidden in the following Bible labyrinth is a verse from the Bible. Start at the top arrow and move one space at a time to the right, left, diagonally, up, or down. You should finish the verse at the bottom arrow.

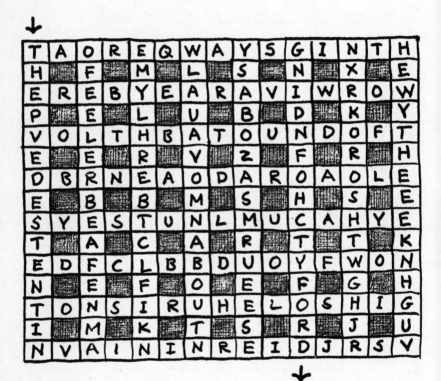

Mixed
Letters

Rearrange the letters to find out who was the father of two of the apostles.

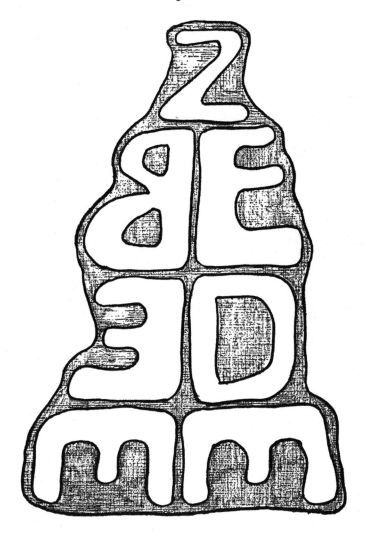

Descriptions
of Hell

The Bible describes hell in several different ways. How many different descriptions can you remember?

1. _____

2. _____

3. _____

4. _____

5. _____

6. _____

7. _____

8. _____

9. _____

10. _____

11. _____

12. _____

13. _____

14. _____

15. _____

16. _____

17. _____

18. _____

19. _____

Resist
The Devil

BEGIN

THE DEVIL

END

And he will flee from you.
James 4:7

Name
The Event

The picture below illustrates a Bible event, story, or verse. Guess which
Bible event, story, or verse the picture is illustrating.

_____

_____

_____

_____

_____

Where in the Bible is this event, story, or verse found? _____

_____

Key Word

To find the key word, fill in the blanks in words 1 through 10 with the missing letters. Transfer those letters to the corresponding numbered squares in the diagram.

1	2	3	4	5	6	7	8	9	10

1. __A E S A R

2. D E A C __ N

3. F __ O C K

4. G L __ R Y

5. I D O L __

6. H A D E __

7. A __ R

8. F __ T H E R

9. B A __ K

10. __ E A

Put Them In Order

Listed below are all of the books of the New Testament.
Place them in proper order on the numbered lines.

II Timothy
II John
Matthew
John
III John
Luke
Mark
II Thessalonians
James
Jude
Philemon
II Corinthians
Titus
I Peter
I Corinthians
Romans
Galatians
Revelation
Philippians
I John
Colossians
Ephesians
I Thessalonians
II Peter
I Timothy
Acts
Hebrews

1. _____
2. _____
3. _____
4. _____
5. _____
6. _____
7. _____
8. _____
9. _____
10. _____
11. _____
12. _____
13. _____
14. _____

15. _____
16. _____
17. _____
18. _____
19. _____
20. _____
21. _____
22. _____
23. _____
24. _____
25. _____
26. _____
27. _____

Cain And Abel
And the Old Men

Genesis 4:1-5:32

1. What was Cain's occupation? _____

2. What was Abel's occupation? _____

3. Who was the first murderer mentioned in the Bible? _____

_____

4. What was the lie Cain told to God? _____

5. What was the name of the land that Cain lived in? _____

_____

6. What was the name of the first city mentioned in the Bible?

_____

7. Who was called the father of all that play the harp and organ?

_____

8. Who was called the instructor of those who work with brass and iron? _____

9. Who was the oldest man mentioned in the Bible? __Lamech

__Adam   __Mahalaleel   __Methuselah   __Samuel

10. How old was the oldest man in the Bible when he died?

_____

11. Match the oldest men mentioned in the Bible with their ages.

A. Adam   ____905

B. Seth   ____895

C. Enos   ____365

D. Cainan   ____930

E. Mahalaleel   ____910

F. Jared   ____969

G. Enoch   ____912

H. Methuselah   ____777

I. Lamech   ____962

12. How many men and women were on the ark? _____
_____

13. Who shut the door to the ark? _____

14. The ark landed on which mountain?

    A. Nebo   D. Everest

    B. Ararat   E. Zion

    C. McKinley

15. What did the dove bring back to Noah? _____

16. How long were Noah and his family in the ark? _____
_____

17. God said something to Noah and his family that was the same thing
he told Adam and Eve. What was it? _____

18. What did Noah do after he left the ark? _____

19. What sign did God give to Noah as a covenant that he would never
again destroy the world by a flood? _____

20. Who was the first man to get drunk in the Bible? _____

Patchword

Like a patchwork quilt, this diagram contains 15 Bible words
or names all mixed up. Two patches form one word.
See if you can piece together this puzzle.

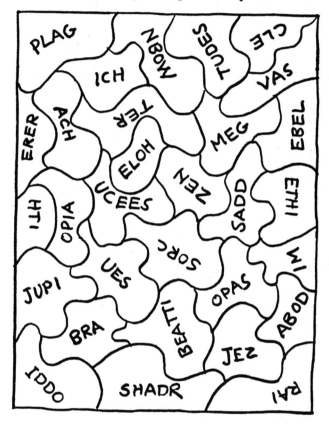

1. _____   6. _____   11. _____

2. _____   7. _____   12. _____

3. _____   8. _____   13. _____

4. _____   9. _____   14. _____

5. _____   10. _____   15. _____

Guess Who

1. Who fell asleep during one of Paul's sermons? _____

2. Who recovered a lost ax? _____

3. Which prophet asked the Lord to turn the sun's shadow back ten degrees? _____

4. Who was the first convert in Europe? _____

5. Who was an eloquent speaker? _____

6. Who had a school in Ephesus? _____

7. Who was a wicked silversmith? _____

8. Who sang when their backs were bleeding? _____

9. Who asked God for wisdom? _____

10. Who was attacked by three armies at one time? _____

11. Who ridiculed Nehemiah? _____

12. Who foiled an assassination plot? _____

13. Who was hung on the gallows he had built to hang someone else? _____

14. Who were Job's comforters? _____

15. Who was envious at the prosperity of the wicked? _____

16. Who said "Woe is me! For I am a man of unclean lips"? _____

17. Who had a vision about a wheel? _____

18. Who was cast into a lions' den? _____

19. Who married a fallen woman by God's order? _____

20. Who went for a ride in a fish? _____

Choose-a-Letter

To discover the Bible verse concealed in the diagram below you will
have to choose a letter. Choose one letter in each pair and draw a line
through the other one to see if you can spell the words in this familiar
Bible verse.

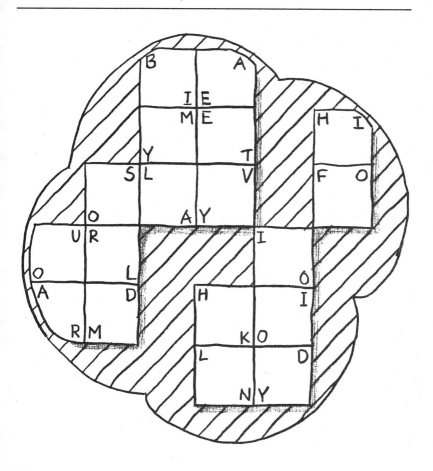

Old Testament Books

In the following word hunt see if you can find 35 of the Old Testament books. Begin with any letter and move one letter at a time to the right, left, up, down, or diagonally. When you have found a word, draw a circle around it.

```
R U D E U T E R O N O M Y J O E L
E S O N G O F S O L O M O N O S A
C A D E N O S H H A B E N O L B M
C M L E M E C H E O A X A P O D E
L U J U D G E S I I D O E Z R A N
E E C A N J O N A H I D N I D N T
S L Z E C H A R I R A U O S X I A
I H A G G A I N O A H S S A A E T
A A L E M I C A H E Z E K I E L I
S B A N J E R E M I A H A A I O O
T A L E V I T I C U S N A H U M N
E K I S P A M O S P R O V E R B S
S K T I M K I N G S S J O S H U A
I U A S Z E P H A N I A H T S O M
N K P S A L M S M A L A C H I O M
N E H E M I A H E N U M B E R S H
G C H R O N I C L E S E E R U T H
```

Skeleton Fill-in

Fit the words supplied into their proper places in the Skeleton Fill-in squares. The words are in alphabetical order according to the number of letters. A word has been entered into the Skeleton Fill-in to help you get started. To proceed, look for a six-letter word having a "T" as the third letter. Continue in this manner until the puzzle is solved.

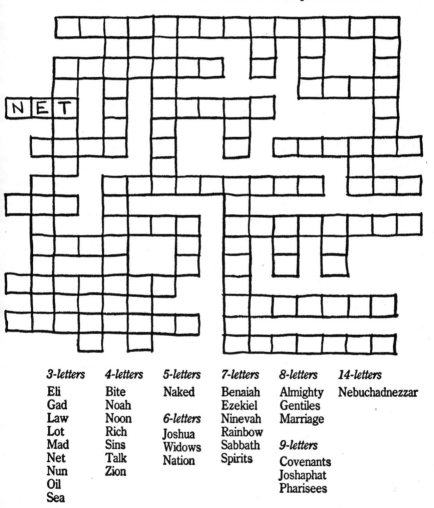

3-letters	4-letters	5-letters	7-letters	8-letters	14-letters
Eli	Bite	Naked	Benaiah	Almighty	Nebuchadnezzar
Gad	Noah		Ezekiel	Gentiles	
Law	Noon	**6-letters**	Ninevah	Marriage	
Lot	Rich	Joshua	Rainbow		
Mad	Sins	Widows	Sabbath	**9-letters**	
Net	Talk	Nation	Spirits	Covenants	
Nun	Zion			Joshaphat	
Oil				Pharisees	
Sea					

Choose-a-Letter

To discover the Bible verse concealed in the diagram below you will have to choose a letter. Choose one letter in each pair and draw a line through the other one and see if you can spell the words in this familiar Bible verse.

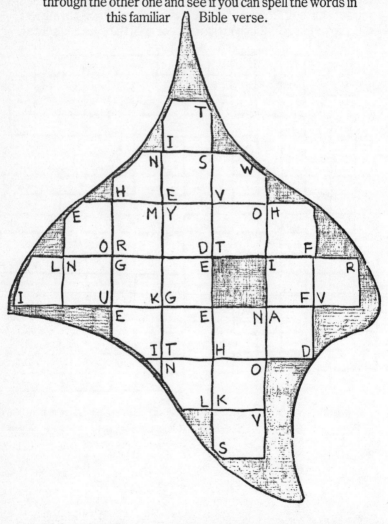

Doctrinal Studies

The term "ology" means "the study of." When it is attached to another word it means the study of the word preceding. Example: Satan + ology = Satanology, or the study of the doctrine of Satan. See how many of the following doctrinal studies you can match.

1. The study of God
2. The study of the Bible
3. The study of Christ
4. The study of angels
5. The study of salvation
6. The study of the church
7. The study of end-time events
8. The study of the Holy Spirit
9. The study of man
10. The study of demons
11. The study of the descent of families

A. Angelology
B. Ecclesiology
C. Theology
D. Bibliology
E. Christology
F. Demonology
G. Genealogy
H. Soteriology
I. Eschatology
J. Pneumatology
K. Anthropology

Tail Tag

Begin at the top arrow and see if you can find a verse from the Bible.
Move one square at a time to the right, left, up, down, or diagonally.
End the verse at the bottom arrow.

Y	L	F	O	R	W	X	P	L	N	O	P	F	J	E	L	Y
J	I	S	A	T	E	F	S	A	M	R	S	I	F	T	H	E
O	Y	A	E	H	N	O	P	Z	A	J	K	S	O	F	A	C
C	H	R	I	E	P	R	E	A	C	H	I	N	G	P	Q	R
Q	Y	T	S	N	P	T	A	H	T	M	E	H	T	O	I	O
D	E	V	A	S	E	B	V	Y	L	F	Q	J	L	T	Z	S
I	R	S	T	L	M	R	I	S	H	O	B	B	I	S	I	S
T	I	S	J	P	Z	D	A	S	N	O	X	S	P	A	J	F
U	V	T	H	E	P	E	X	O	P	L	W	M	T	C	O	S
Q	D	A	F	O	F	V	H	R	Q	I	U	S	I	K	L	G
O	P	T	W	W	A	W	E	Y	I	S	P	L	F	P	I	O
I	S	E	T	H	S	U	O	F	I	H	Z	A	E	M	G	D
A	R	O	F	A	B	Q	T	J	B	N	W	M	D	C	H	R
L	N	G	R	S	T	D	N	K	O	E	I	N	R	I	T	I
P	O	Z	I	C	A	B	U	B	A	S	C	J	O	Q	S	E
D	K	J	H	L	M	Q	T	U	B	S	R	Y	L	P	A	H
Z	E	B	R	A	S	L	I	K	E	T	O	W	A	L	K	T

Jumbles

Unscramble the names of four men mentioned in the Bible. The letters in the parenthesis marks now form a new scrambled name of a man from the Bible. See if you can discover all of these important men.

SCRAMBLED NAME	UNSCRAMBLED NAME
1. M J A E S	( )_( )__
A N R B A B A S	( )__( )_____
S R I A L E	( )__( )( )_
M I N O R D	( )_____

New scrambled name ( )( )( )( )( )( )( )( )

Unscrambled name _____

2. Y R C U S	__( )__
M A H	( )( )_
A O J N H	_( )_( )( )
U A L P	( )___

New scrambled name ( )( )( )( )( )( )( )

Unscrambled name _____

A Quote From Gideon

Start at the arrow and move one square at a time in any direction. You may move to the right, left, up or down, or diagonally, but do not cross any letter twice. All letters must be used to discover the quote from Gideon.

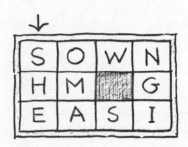

_____

_____

The Attributes Of God

When we speak of the attributes of God we are referring to God's essence, substance, being, nature, qualities, characteristics, or disposition. How many attributes of God can you identify.
Example: God is love.

1. _____
2. _____
3. _____
4. _____
5. _____
6. _____
7. _____
8. _____
9. _____
10. _____
11. _____
12. _____
13. _____
14. _____
15. _____
16. _____
17. _____
18. _____
19. _____
20. _____
21. _____
22. _____
23. _____
24. _____
25. _____
26. _____
27. _____
28. _____
29. _____
30. _____
31. _____
32. _____
33. _____
34. _____
35. _____
36. _____

Name
The Event

The picture below illustrates a Bible event, story, or verse.
Guess which Bible event, story, or verse the picture is illustrating.

_____

_____

_____

_____

_____

Where in the Bible is this event, story, or verse found? _____

_____

Quotation Puzzle

In the puzzle below, you are to fit the letters in each column into the boxes directly above them. The letters may or may not go into the boxes in the same order in which they are given. It is up to you to decide which letter goes into which box above it. Once a letter is used, cross it off the bottom half of the diagram and do not use it again. In the puzzle, some letters have been entered into the diagram as an aid to you, and those letters have been crossed off. A black square indicates the end of a word. When the diagram is filled in, you will be able to find the completed quotation by reading across the boxes.

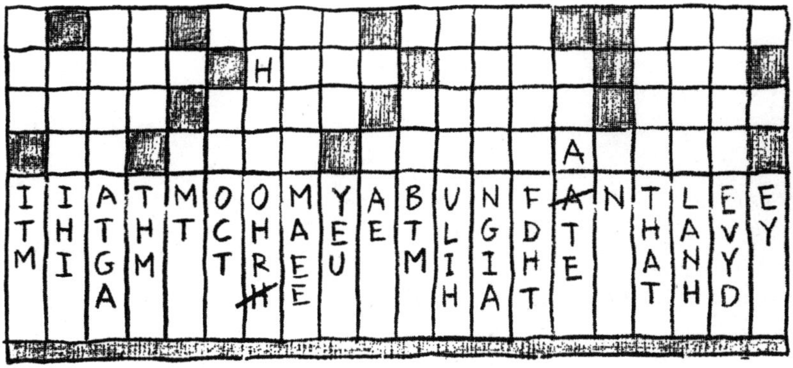

Letters to place (by column):

I	I	A	T	M	O	O	M	Y	A	B	U	N	F	A	N	T	L	E	E
T	H	T	H	T	C	H	A	E	E	T	L	G	D	T		H	A	V	Y
M	I	G	M		T	R	E	U		M	I	I	H	E		A	N	V	
		A				E	E				H	A	T			T	H	D	

(Given letters already placed in the grid: **H** and **A** in the upper boxes; **R**, **A** crossed off below.)

Versigram

See if you can unscramble the following familiar Bible verses.

1. ndA uhot htlas vloe eht dLor hyt odG ihtw lla ineth tareh, adn whit

_____

lal yht ulos, dan thiw lla yth tmigh.

2. rFo eroth unfoonitad nac on mna yla nhta ttah si dlai, hhicw

_____

si ssueJ stiChr.

_____

3. oGd si uor furege dna tnegthsr, a ervy tnseerp plhe ni rotulbe.

_____

4. sA ey avhe reeeorfth cereidev tsCrhi eussJ hte dLor, os klwa ey

_____

ni mhi: ooRetd dna ublti pu ni mih, dan blstaisdeh ni eth hitaf,
sa ey vahe eebn ttghua, unboagind inereht thiw ksthgiangniv.

_____

5. heT tttsaues fo het doLr era ghtir, joercigni hte eahrt: eth

_____

ocmmmanentd of het dorL is uper, ginnethgilne eth syee.

_____

Temptation And Fall of Man

Genesis 3:1-4:3

1. Of all the animals God created, the ＿＿＿＿＿＿＿ was the most subtle.

2. The ＿＿＿＿＿＿ told Eve that she would not ＿＿＿＿＿＿.

3. The ＿＿＿＿＿＿＿ said that if Eve would eat the forbidden fruit she would:

    A. Become wealthy   D. Become smart

    B. Become more healthy   E. Become as gods

    C. Become powerful

4. What was the first thing that happened to Adam and Eve when they ate the forbidden fruit? ＿＿＿＿＿＿＿＿＿＿＿

5. What was the first thing Adam and Eve did after eating the forbidden fruit? ＿＿＿＿＿＿＿＿＿＿＿

6. What was the first thing Adam and Eve did when they heard the voice of God while walking in the garden? ＿＿＿＿＿＿＿

＿＿＿＿＿＿＿＿＿＿＿＿＿＿＿＿＿＿＿＿＿

Where did they do this? ＿＿＿＿＿＿＿＿＿＿＿

7. What was the first thing God said to Adam and Eve after they ate the forbidden fruit?

    A. Why did you do it?   D. You were wrong for eating.

    B. Where art thou?   E. You will be punished.

    C. Now you shall die.   F. Why are you hiding?

8. Whom did Eve blame for causing her to eat the forbidden fruit?

_____

9. Whom did Adam blame for causing him to eat the forbidden fruit?

_____

10. What did God do to the serpent?

    A. Caused him to die

    B. Made him crawl on his belly

    C. Banished him from the garden

11. When did Adam first call his wife Eve?

    A. Before the fall

    B. During the fall

    C. After the fall

12. As a result of the fall, women have sorrow and pain in childbirth.

_____ True   _____ False

13. As a result of the fall, man has to work by the sweat of his brow.

_____ True   _____ False

14. What did God make for Adam and Eve? _____

_____

15. God made Adam and Eve do something for eating the forbidden fruit. What was it? _____

16. Why couldn't Adam and Eve go in and out of the Garden of Eden? _____

17. The name of Adam and Eve's first child was _____.

18. The name of Adam and Eve's second child was _____.

Name
The Event

The picture below illustrates a Bible event, story, or verse.
Guess which Bible event, story, or verse the picture is illustrating.

_____

_____

_____

_____

_____

Where in the Bible is this event, story, or verse found? _____

_____

Alphagram

Twenty-six words from the Bible are hidden in the diagram on the opposite page. See if you can find them all. One letter is missing from each word. The missing letter may be at the beginning, ending, or anyplace within the word. As you fill in the diagram you will find that there are 26 missing letters. . . . one letter for each letter of the alphabet. Since a letter will be used only once, an alphabetical listing has been provided for your assistance. As you use a letter in the diagram, cross it off the alphabetical list.

A B C D E F G H I

J K L M N O P Q R

S T U V W X Y Z

M	E	S	N	O		A	J	U	R	O
A	M	A	M	P		O	A	H	B	N
S	A	Z	L	J		B	T	Q	A	S
E	O	K	P	I		O	M	A	N	D
R	T	S	T	E		H	E	N	S	J
P	S	A	H	A		K	T	E	I	E
T	Y	O	B	B		A	R	T	Y	R
N	J	N	P	R		N	C	E	R	M
B	C	H	E	R		B	C	A	S	S
M	I	M	G	R		E	K	C	P	H
O	C	L	C	H		U	D	E	S	P
F	O	G	D	E		O	T	E	D	O
L	F	A	L	E		A	N	D	E	R
A	Q	U	I	L		L	U	B	N	D
J	X	E	D	S		O	D	O	M	G
E	A	R	T	H		U	A	K	E	L
N	D	K	R	E		O	V	E	F	S
E	P	J	F	O		A	D	I	A	H
H	C	E	L	E		T	V	E	O	M
B	S	I	E	C		R	U	S	G	L
L	M	G	D	M		I	S	S	J	N
M	R	H	W	N		I	D	E	O	N
R	L	J	T	I		U	S	H	S	K
I	P	P	S	A		M	S	F	I	D
A	O	P	E	R		E	C	T	S	C
L	B	G	F	K		E	A	R	T	J

BIBLE FUN

Key Word

To find the key word, fill in the blanks in words 1 through 10 with the correct missing letters. Transfer those letters to the corresponding numbered squares in the diagram.

1	2	3	4	5	6	7	8	9	10

1. G I __ T
2. F L __ O D
3. H A G A __
4. C A M __ L
5. H O U __

6. H O __ S E
7. A G O __ Y
8. G E __ E S I S
9. B __ A S T
10. D O O __

Escape From
The Circle of Sin

Put Them In Order

Listed below are all of the books of the Old Testament. Place them in their proper order.

Esther Jonah Joel Exodus Habakkuk Lamentations I Chronicles I Kings Proverbs I Samuel Zephaniah Judges Deuteronomy Genesis Ruth Ecclesiastes Haggai Amos Daniel Song of Solomon Ezra Joshua Hosea Zechariah Obadiah Micah Isaiah Ezekiel Leviticus Psalms Numbers Malachi II Chronicles Nahum II Samuel II Kings Jeremiah Job Nehemiah

1. _____	14. _____	27. _____
2. _____	15. _____	28. _____
3. _____	16. _____	29. _____
4. _____	17. _____	30. _____
5. _____	18. _____	31. _____
6. _____	19. _____	32. _____
7. _____	20. _____	33. _____
8. _____	21. _____	34. _____
9. _____	22. _____	35. _____
10. _____	23. _____	36. _____
11. _____	24. _____	37. _____
12. _____	25. _____	38. _____
13. _____	26. _____	39. _____

Abraham

Genesis 12:1-23:20

1. What was Abraham's name before it was changed? _____
   _____

2. What was Sarah's name before it was changed? _____
   _____

3. What was the name of Abraham's nephew? _____
   _____

4. What was the name of the King of Salem that Abraham met after rescuing his nephew?

   A. Manasseh   C. Marduk

   B. Menahem   D. Melchizedek

5. What was the name of Sarah's handmaid? _____

6. What was the name of Abraham's first son, who was born of Sarah's handmaid? _____
   _____

7. Abraham was _____ years old when his son Isaac was born.

8. God supplied a sacrifice for Abraham to offer other than his own son. What was it?

   A. A goat   C. A sheep

   B. A ram   D. A calf

9. How many times did Abraham ask God to spare the city of Sodom?

   A. 2 times   C. 6 times

   B. 4 times   D. 8 times

10. Abraham was called a _____ of God.

11. When Sarah heard that she was going to have a child in her old age she _____ .

12. How many sons _____ and daughters _____ did Lot have?

13. Two things rained on Sodom and Gomorrah. What were they? _____ and _____

14. What happened to Lot's wife? _____

15. Abraham did not cast out Sarah's bondwoman and her son.
    _____ True _____ False

16. God told Abraham that He would make him a _____ . _____

17. Sarah was _____ years old when she died.

18. Abraham told a lie when he said that Sarah was his sister. How many times did he do this? __ 1 __ 2 __ 3 __ 4 __ 5

19. Sarah was actually:

    A. No sister to Abraham

    B. A sister by adoption

    C. A sister by birth

    D. A half sister

20. How old was Abraham when he died?

    A. 127

    B. 152

    C. 169

    D. 175

Names and Titles of Jesus

In the following word hunt find 41 names and titles of Jesus.
Begin with any letter and move one letter at a time
to the right, left, up, down, or diagonally. When you have found
a word, draw a circle around it.

```
A  I  M  M  A  N  U  E  L  B  M  Y  O  W  L  P  I
M  E  D  I  A  P  Q  W  C  S  T  L  M  G  O  D  A
R  A  N  S  O  M  R  A  L  P  H  A  E  L  G  R  M
I  L  L  I  G  H  T  Y  D  O  G  S  G  O  O  B  D
G  I  A  I  C  H  R  I  S  E  V  T  A  A  S  I  B
H  S  M  P  F  M  U  J  R  L  I  O  D  F  E  S  H
T  A  B  W  X  E  T  P  A  M  N  R  L  F  A  H  I
E  J  E  S  U  S  H  G  B  R  E  A  D  I  R  O  G
O  U  S  I  T  S  N  Y  Z  H  D  M  A  R  O  P  H
U  D  C  H  R  I  S  T  P  T  O  E  R  S  C  N  P
S  G  K  R  K  A  M  E  N  O  O  D  K  T  K  J  R
O  E  M  U  C  H  H  G  O  P  R  I  N  C  E  K  I
N  L  A  P  O  S  T  L  E  M  Y  A  J  T  R  U  E
E  A  D  V  O  C  A  T  E  D  O  T  B  O  B  L  S
P  R  O  P  H  E  T  S  A  V  I  O  U  R  I  O  T
M  E  P  O  T  E  N  T  A  T  E  R  C  A  N  R  R
A  L  M  I  G  H  T  Y  H  O  L  Y  O  N  E  D  E
```

Name
The Event

The picture below illustrates a Bible event, story or verse.
Guess which Bible event, story or verse the picture is illustrating.

_____

_____

_____

_____

_____

Where in the Bible is this event, story, or verse found? _____

_____

A Place
For Every One

Can you find a place for every one of the five-letter names of the Bible
characters listed below? One individual has already been given a place.
The letter in the dark square can be used more than once.

Aaron	Geuel	Massa	Regem
Abdon	Gibea	Moses	Reuel
Abiel	Isaac	Naham	Rhoda
Amasa	Jeuel	Orpha	Rufus
Amram	Judas	Peter	Sheba
Attai	Laban	Rahab	
Barak	Ludim		

Gifts of
the Spirit

How many of the gifts of the Spirit from
I Corinthians 12:4-11 and Romans 12:6-8
can you remember?

1. _____

2. _____

3. _____

4. _____

5. _____

6. _____

7. _____

8. _____

9. _____

10. _____

11. _____

12. _____

13. _____

14. _____

15. _____

Bible
Labyrinth

Hidden in the following Bible labyrinth is a verse from the Bible. Start at the top arrow and move one space at a time to the right, left, up, or down. You should finish the verse at the bottom arrow.

W	S	A	S	E	R	E	A	R	C	G	E	S	R	O
E	A	A	H	F	Q	Z	Y	I
H	A	V	E	T	D	O	B	P	L	I	A	L	M	K
F	X	Y	R	Z	C	L	N
T	R	O	P	P	O	E	S	L	M	E	N	Y	U	N
U	I	J	A	K	P	X	T
N	I	T	Y	L	B	M	E	N	E	S	O	W	T	O
G	H	E	L	J	P	V	T
O	D	S	U	T	C	L	I	E	S	U	Q	M	E	H
G	E	D	A	H	O	W	U
O	O	D	U	N	T	O	H	O	R	H	S	H	O	A
K	F	G	Y	L	E	U	R
C	E	O	E	A	F	F	O	D	T	H	T	F	O	E
W	H	I	Z	A	V	W	X
N	R	U	O	T	H	J	F	D	H	J	B	L	M	O

Jumbles

Unscramble the names of four men mentioned in the Bible. The letters in parenthesis now form a new scrambled name of a man from the Bible. See if you can discover all of these important men.

SCRAMBLED NAME   UNSCRAMBLED NAME

1. G A G A   _ ( ) _ _

   S U P P I H L R A   ( ) _ _ _ _ _ ( ) ( ) _ _

   N N A A S I A   _ _ _ _ _ ( ) _ _

   B N A R E   ( ) _ _ _ _ ( )

   New scrambled name   ( )( )( )( )( )( )( )

   Unscrambled name _ _ _ _ _ _ _

2. Q U A A L I   ( ) _ _ _ _ _ ( )

   M O S A   _ ( ) _ _

   Z O R A   ( ) _ _ ( )

   K B K A H A U K   ( ) _ ( ) _ _ _ _ _

   New scrambled name   ( )( )( )( )( )( )( )

   Unscrambled name _ _ _ _ _ _ _

Key Word

To find the key word, fill in the blanks in words 1 through 10 with the correct missing letters. Transfer those letters to the corresponding numbered squares in the diagram.

1	2	3	4	5	6	7	8	9	10

1. C A R __

2. P __ A C E

3. A L __ S

4. __ O T

5. M A S __ E R

6. B E __ R D

7. D E S E R __

8. N A Z A R __ T E

9. E N __ C H

10. G I A __ T

B I B L E   F U N

Patchword

Like a patchwork quilt, this diagram contains fifteen Bible words or names all mixed up. Two patches form one word. See if you can piece together this puzzle.

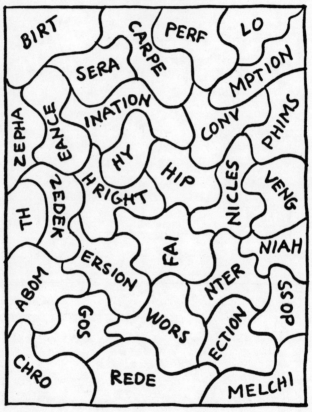

1. _____   6. _____   11. _____

2. _____   7. _____   12. _____

3. _____   8. _____   13. _____

4. _____   9. _____   14. _____

5. _____   10. _____   15. _____

Alphanumber

There are numbers in each square of the diagram below. The numbers represent letters of the alphabet. Change the numbers to letters and discover an important Bible thought.

A B C D E F G H I J K L M N
1 2 3 4 5 6 7 8 9 10 11 12 13 14

O P Q R S T U V W X Y Z SPACE
15 16 17 18 19 20 21 22 23 24 25 26 27

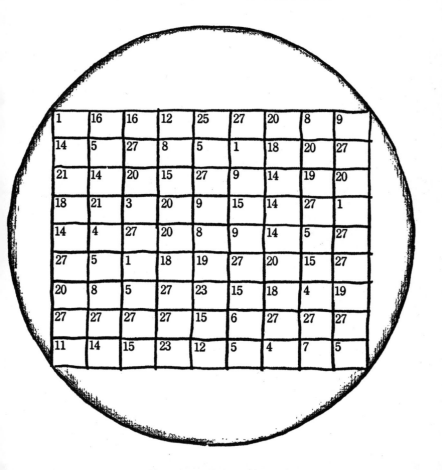

Noah And The Flood

Genesis 6:1 — 9:29

1. God became angry with sinful men and gave them _____ years to live.

2. Noah found _____ in the eyes of the Lord.

3. The names of Noah's three sons were _____ , _____ , and _____ .

4. God told Noah to make an ark out of what kind of wood?

    A. Oak

    B. Gopher

    C. Cedar

    D. Ash

5. God told Noah to put something on the inside and outside of the Ark. What was it? _____

6. The size of the ark was to be _____ cubits long, _____ wide, and _____ cubits high.

7. How many windows were in the ark?

    ___ 1 ___ 3 ___ 5 ___ 7

8. How many stories were in the ark? ___ 1 ___ 2 ___ 3 ___ 4

9. How many of each kind of animal did Noah take into the ark? (Be careful of your answer) _____

10. How many days and nights did God cause it to rain? _____

_____

11. How old was Noah when he entered the ark?

     A. 200

     B. 300

     C. 400

     D. 500

     E. 600

12. How many men and women were on the ark? _____

13. Who shut the door to the ark? _____

14. The ark landed on which mountain?

     A. Nebo

     B. Ararat

     C. McKinley

     D. Everest

     E. Zion

15. What did the dove bring back to Noah? _____

16. How long were Noah and his family in the ark? _____

17. God said something to Noah and his family that was the same thing he told Adam and Eve. What was it? _____

18. What did Noah do after he left the Ark? _____

_____

19. What sign did God give to Noah as a covenant that he would never again destroy the world by a flood? _____

20. Who was the first man to get drunk in the Bible? _____

_____

The Escape From Darkness to Light

START

FINISH

Famous People Match

Match the letter of each occupation or
accomplishment to the correct individual
on the left.

1. Ishmael	A. Prophetess
2. Nimrod	B. Judge
3. Esau	C. Fisherman
4. Paul	D. Slayer with jaw bone
5. Peter	E. Cunning hunter
6. Matthew	F. Angel
7. Saul	G. Pharisee
8. David	H. Queen
9. Simon	I. High priest
10. Esther	J. Wall builder
11. Deborah	K. Archer
12. Anna	L. Tentmaker
13. Gabriel	M. King
14. Nicodemus	N. Magician
15. Nehemiah	O. Giant killer
16. Aaron	P. Tax collector
17. Lydia	Q. Mighty hunter
18. Pilate	R. Prophet
19. Micah	S. Purple cloth seller
20. Samson	T. Governor

A Quote
From Ruth

Start at the arrow and move one square at a time in any direction. You may move to the right, left, up, down, or diagonally, but do not cross any letter twice. All the letters must be used to discover the quote from Ruth.

	T	P	E	M	Y	Y	G
H	Y	E	B	P	E	H	O
L	O	L	P	O	T	D	M
P	E	L	L	E	D	G	Y
S	H	A	A	N	O	D	

_____

_____

_____

Name
The Event

The picture below illustrates a Bible event, story, or verse. Try to guess which Bible event, story or verse the picture is illustrating.

_____

_____

_____

_____

_____

_____

Where in the Bible is this event, story, or verse found? _____

_____

Odd
Or Even

To find out the name of the leader of an army that attacked Joshua, cross out all the letters with the even numbers. Three false letters have been inserted to confuse you. Watch out.

Joseph

Genesis
41:1 — 50:26

MATCH THE FOLLOWING:

1. The youngest son of Jacob

2. The second chariot

3. Hidden in the sack of food

4. Joseph

5. Zaphnath-Paaneah

6. Shepherds

7. The place where Jacob was buried

8. Seven fat and seven lean cattle

9. The place where God speaks to Jacob

10. Asenath

11. Dwelling place for Joseph's family

12. Manasseh and Ephraim

A. A dream of Pharaoh

B. The wife Pharaoh gave Joseph

C. The name Pharaoh gave Joseph

D. Goshen

E. Beersheba

F. The sons of Joseph

G. Wept aloud

H. Benjamin

I. An abomination to the Egyptians

J. Something Joseph rode

K. The field of Machpelah

L. Silver cup

Mixed
Letters

Rearrange the letters to find out who said, "Behold, the Lamb of God."

Clusters

How many Bible women can you find in the lines below?
The letters may or may not overlap.

1. JERUSHABIGAILEAHERODIASARAHCORNELIADINAH

2. EUNICEVEDAMARISAPPHIRANNABILHAHDORCASALOME

3. ORPAHZILPAHABISHAGDURSILLAVASHTIJEZEBELMARY

4. GOMERACHELYDIABERNICESTHERUTHNNATAMARHODA

Help Paul and Silas Escape

Starting at the "X" in the inner prison, help the apostles find their way to freedom.

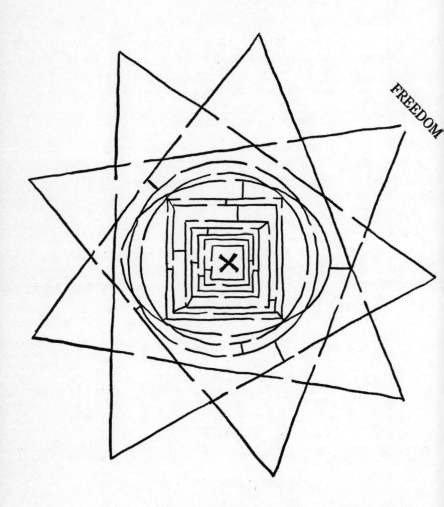

Things
God Hates

In Proverbs 6:16-19 God lists seven things that he hates. Do you know what they are?

1. _____

2. _____

3. _____

4. _____

5. _____

6. _____

7. _____

Bible Labyrinth

Hidden in the following Bible labyrinth is a verse from the Bible. Start at the top arrow and move one space at a time to the right, left, up, down, or diagonally. You should finish the verse at the bottom arrow.

F	E	R	P	Y	H	C	O	I	O	S	E	N	E	G
O	E	O	E	B	E	T	D
R	A	H	T	U	B	E	S	E	N	R	C	Y	O	U
E	J	I	C	F	P	A	R
B	R	E	T	H	H	H	A	T	Y	E	F	D	O	B
L	Q	R	T	E	Z	I	B
T	Y	B	N	E	K	D	D	C	I	F	G	E	S	A
H	R	M	O	E	I	H	L
E	S	E	S	O	F	G	M	H	I	R	C	A	O	I
M	I	L	Y	O	X	S	Y
E	R	C	K	I	H	W	D	L	Y	A	C	G	N	I
T	U	C	J	O	W	C	N
O	Y	S	I	H	N	A	B	G	O	T	N	E	P	T
U	V	O	B	L	I	U	A
R	R	E	A	S	L	E	S	E	R	V	C	E	L	B

A Quote From Adam

Start at the arrow and move one square at a time in any direction. You may move to the right, left, up, down, or diagonally, but do not cross any letter twice. All the letters must be used to discover the quote from Adam.

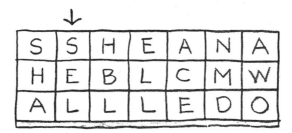

S	S	H	E	A	N	A
H	E	B	L	C	M	W
A	L	L	L	E	D	O

_____

_____

Anticipation

In eleven moves see if you can discover something that every Christian should look forward to.

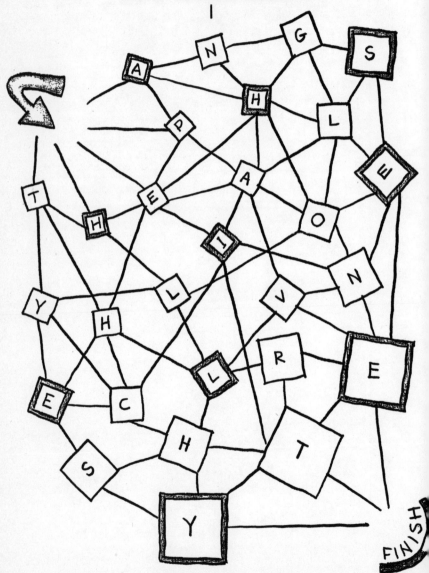

A Place For Every One

Can you find a place for every one of the three-letter names of Bible characters listed below? One individual has already been given a place. The letter in the dark square can be used more than once.

Abi	Dan	Gog	Iru	Pul
Ahi	Eli	Hod	Lyu	Ram
Ara	Eve	Hur	Ner	Zur
Ard	Gad	Ira	Nun	

Ten Commandments

Can you complete the Ten Commandments?

1. Thou shalt have _____

   _____

2. Thou shalt not make _____

   _____

3. Thou shall not take _____

   _____

4. Remember _____

   _____

5. Honor _____

   _____

6. Thou shalt not _____

   _____

7. Thou shalt not _____

   _____

8. Thou shalt not _____

   _____

9. Thou shalt not _____

   _____

10. Thou shalt not _____

    _____

David's
Scroll

David's scroll has been rolled up so that you can't read all the words. Can you finish the sentences without taking time to unroll the scroll?

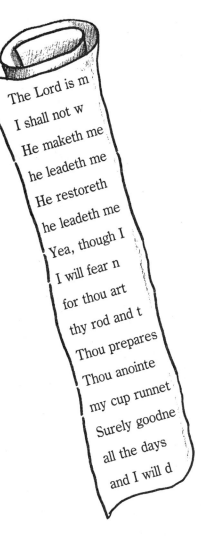

The Lord is m

I shall not w

He maketh me

he leadeth me

He restoreth

he leadeth me

Yea, though I

I will fear n

for thou art

thy rod and t

Thou prepares

Thou anointe

my cup runnet

Surely goodne

all the days

and I will d

Names and Designations For Satan

In the following word hunt find 29 names and designations for Satan.
Begin with any letter and move one letter at a time to the right, left,
up, down, or diagonally. When you have found a word, draw a circle
around it.

```
E  A  N  G  E  L  O  F  T  H  E  A  B  Y  S  S  O
A  G  O  O  D  L  M  U  R  D  E  R  E  R  R  T  F
D  S  M  I  W  I  C  K  E  D  O  N  E  L  O  H  A
V  O  P  P  R  E  S  S  O  R  M  N  E  O  A  I  T
E  B  L  E  V  I  A  T  H  A  N  T  H  V  R  E  H
R  D  E  V  I  L  S  I  T  I  N  M  O  E  I  F  E
S  E  S  E  L  I  K  E  S  E  N  E  M  Y  N  S  R
A  C  A  S  L  I  A  R  P  Z  W  C  A  N  G  A  O
R  E  T  W  K  Z  K  R  R  B  J  O  U  Y  L  P  F
Y  I  A  E  I  T  E  M  P  T  E  R  L  T  I  O  L
E  V  N  E  N  S  O  B  E  L  I  A  L  F  O  L  I
R  E  K  T  D  A  C  C  U  S  E  R  I  O  N  L  E
D  R  A  G  O  N  M  E  F  B  N  I  C  E  S  Y  S
S  T  R  O  N  G  M  A  N  L  A  B  A  D  D  O  N
C  H  E  R  U  B  J  G  O  D  O  F  A  G  E  N  K
A  P  O  W  E  R  O  F  D  A  R  K  N  E  S  S  I
C  P  R  I  N  C  E  O  F  D  E  M  O  N  S  L  L
```

Name
The Event

The picture below illustrates a Bible event, story, or verse.
Try to guess which Bible event, story, or verse the picture is
illustrating.

_____

_____

_____

_____

_____

Where in the Bible is this event, story, or verse found? _____

_____

Help Jonah
Escape

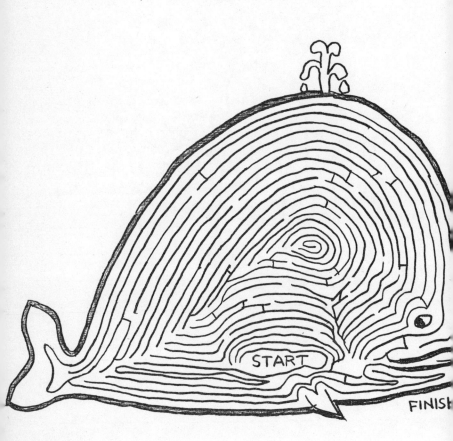

START

FINISH

Adam and Eve

Genesis 2:4 — 2:25

1. God formed man from the

    A. Mud   B. Clay   C. Hard soil   D. Dust

2. What did God do to make man a living soul? _____

    _____

3. What was the name of God's garden? _____

4. What were the names of two special trees that God planted in His

    garden? _____ and _____

5. What went out of the Garden that had four heads? _____

    _____

6. What were the names of the four heads? 1. _____

    2. _____ 3. _____

    4. _____

7. What job did God give to man? _____

8. God told man not to eat of the tree of the knowledge of good and

    evil because he would:

    A. Get sick   B. Break out in sores   C. Die   D. Throw up

9. Who gave names to every living creature?

    ____ God   ____ Adam and Eve   ____ Eve   ____ Adam

10. How did God make the first woman? _____

11. What did Adam first call Eve? _____

12. God said that all of the things He created were good. He did say, however, that one thing was not good. What was that one thing?

_____

Name
The Event

The picture below illustrates a Bible event, story, or verse. Try to guess which Bible event, story, or verse the picture is illustrating.

_____

_____

_____

_____

_____

Where in the Bible is this event, story or verse found? _____

_____

Alphanumber

There are numbers in each square of the diagram below. The numbers represent letters of the alphabet. Change the numbers to letters and discover an important Bible thought.

A	B	C	D	E	F	G	H	I
1	2	3	4	5	6	7	8	9

J	K	L	M	N	O	P	Q	R
10	11	12	13	14	15	16	17	18

S	T	U	V	W	X	Y	Z	SPACE
19	20	21	22	23	24	25	26	27

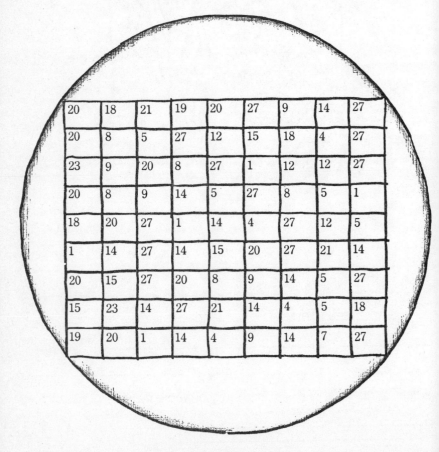

20	18	21	19	20	27	9	14	27
20	8	5	27	12	15	18	4	27
23	9	20	8	27	1	12	12	27
20	8	9	14	5	27	8	5	1
18	20	27	1	14	4	27	12	5
1	14	27	14	15	20	27	21	14
20	15	27	20	8	9	14	5	27
15	23	14	27	21	14	4	5	18
19	20	1	14	4	9	14	7	27

The Circle of Love

- How many circles are there in the puzzle? _____
- How many times is the letter "L" used? _____
- How many times is the letter "O" used? _____
- How many times is the letter "V" used? _____
- How many times is the letter "E" used? _____
- How many circles contain the letter "L"? _____
- How many circles contain the letter "O"? _____
- How many circles contain the letter "V"? _____
- How many circles contain the letter "E"? _____

Joseph

Genesis 37:1 — 40:23

1. Jacob loved Reuben more than Joseph._____ True _____ False

2. Joseph shared a dream with his brothers that they did not like.

   _____ True _____ False

3. Joseph shared a second dream with his brothers in which the sun and moon and 12 stars bowed down to him.

   _____ True _____ False

4. Joseph went in search of his brothers and found them in a place called Dothan. _____ True _____ False

5. Joseph had a coat that had many _____ in it.

6. Joseph's brothers plotted to kill him but his brother _____ talked them out of it.

7. Joseph's brothers sold him to the _____ merchants for_____ pieces of silver.

8. Joseph's brothers told Jacob that Joseph was killed by _____ .

9. The merchants sold Joseph in Egypt to a captain of Pharaoh's guard named _____.

10. Joseph was cast into prison under some false charges. In prison Joseph met two men who had worked for the Pharaoh. One was the Pharaoh's chief _____ , and the other was Pharaoh's chief _____.

11. Which of the two men in prison with Joseph was restored to his former position by Pharaoh? _____

Odd
or Even

Hidden in this odd or even is an instruction from the book of I Thessalonians. See if you can discover what it is. Cross out all of the letters with odd numbers. Then rearrange the letters to discover this instruction from the Bible.

Houses for the Scholar

See if you can match the meanings of the following houses with the proper name.

1. House of the Lord	A. Bethemek
2. House of poverty	B. Bethcar
3. House of the desert	C. Bethgader
4. House of vanity	D. Bethesda
5. House of unripe figs	E. Bethgamul
6. House of my creation	F. Bethhaccerem
7. House of sheep	G. Bethharan
8. House of fig cakes	H. Bethbarah
9. House of God	I. Bethany
10. House of the valley	J. Betharabah
11. House of mercy	K. Bethaven
12. House of the wall	L. Bethphage
13. House of recompence	M. Bethhogla
14. House of the vineyard	N. Bethleaphrah
15. House of the mountain	O. Bethlebaoth
16. House of a partridge	P. Bethlehem
17. House of dust	Q. Bethsaida
18. House of lionesses	R. Bethbiri
19. House of bread	S. Bethdiblathaim
20. House of fishing	T. Bethel

Typeology

A Biblical "type" is a divinely designed illustration of some truth. A type may be a person, an event, a thing, an institution, or a ceremony. How many types can you identify.

1. Adam	A. A type of the Holy Spirit
2. Amalek	B. A type of righteous judgment
3. Ark	C. A type of sin
4. Blue	D. A type of Christ
5. Brass	E. A type of the flesh
6. Candlestick	F. A type of salvation
7. Rock	G. A type of Heaven
8. Lamb	H. A type of judgment
9. Fig leaves	I. A type of evil teaching
10. Fire	J. A type of strength and power
11. Horn	K. A type of human righteousness
12. Leprosy	L. A type of grace and mercy
13. Leaven	M. A type of joy
14. Lion	N. A type of the Word of God
15. Oil	O. A type of power, strength and honor
16. Rainbow	
17. Wine	
18. Hammer	
19. Water	
20. Sword	

Skeleton
Fill-in

Fit the words supplied into their proper places in the Skeleton Fill-In squares. The words are in alphabetical order according to the number of letters. A word has been entered into the Skeleton Fill-In to help you get started. To proceed, look for a three-letter word that ends in "D." Continue in this manner until the puzzle is solved.

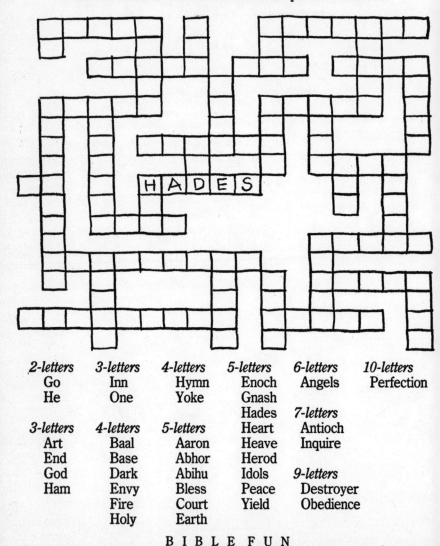

2-letters	3-letters	4-letters	5-letters	6-letters	10-letters
Go	Inn	Hymn	Enoch	Angels	Perfection
He	One	Yoke	Gnash		
			Hades	7-letters	
3-letters	4-letters	5-letters	Heart	Antioch	
Art	Baal	Aaron	Heave	Inquire	
End	Base	Abhor	Herod		
God	Dark	Abihu	Idols	9-letters	
Ham	Envy	Bless	Peace	Destroyer	
	Fire	Court	Yield	Obedience	
	Holy	Earth			

Seals, Trumpets
And Vials

In the book of Revelation the apostle John mentions the various seal, trumpet, and vial judgments. Can you match the proper event with the proper seal, trumpet, or vial judgment?

1. Fourth seal

2. Sun and moon darkened

3. Third seal

4. Rivers and springs turn to blood

5. Fire and blood

6. Army of 200,000,000

7. Malignant sores

8. Second seal

9. Darkness

10. Burning mountain thrown into sea

11. Locusts with scorpion stings

12. Sixth seal

13. Great hailstorm, mighty earthquake

14. Frog spirits

15. First seal

16. Oceans turn to blood

17. Flaming star falling, bitterness

18. Increased heat of the sun

19. Islands and mountains vanish

20. Fifth seal

A. Second trumpet

B. Sixth trumpet

C. War

D. Seventh trumpet

E. Second vial

F. Fifth vial

G. Conquering horse
   and rider

H. Third trumpet

I. Persecution

J. First vial

K. Sixth vial

L. Fifth trumpet

M. Famine

N. Seventh vial

O. First trumpet

P. Third vial

Q. Death

R. Fourth trumpet

S. Fourth vial

T. Destruction

Clusters

How many Bible women can you find in the lines below? The letters may or may not overlap.

1. ZILLAHCANDACEPRISCILLANAOMIPHOEBEJO

2. HAGARZIPPORAHMARTHAJOCHEBEDELILAHKETURA

3. SAPPHIRAMIRIAMICHALOISUSANNAELISABETHCHLOE

HAKEBEREBEOHPHAROB

4. CLAUDIARAHABATHSHEBAJUPITHDEB

Creation

Genesis 1:1 — 2:3

1. What are the first two things God created?

   1. _____ 2. _____

2. God said: A. "Let there be trees."

   B. "Let there be animals."

   C. "Let there be light."

   D. "Let there be creeping things."

3. God divided the water from water. _____ True _____ False

4. What did God call the firmament? _____

5. What moved over the water? _____

6. What did God call the dry land? _____

7. God called the water by what name? _____

8. On which day of creation did God make grass and trees?

   A. second

   B. third

   C. fourth

   D. fifth

9. On which day did God create great whales? _____

10. God created creeping things on the fourth day.

    _____ True _____ False

11. What did God think about all of His creation? _____

12. What did God do on the seventh day?

13. Match the creation days with what was created:

A. Day one   _____ Creeping things

B. Day two   _____ Light

C. Day three   _____ Winged fowl

D. Day four   _____ Tree yielding fruit

E. Day five   _____ Man

F. Day six   _____ Nothing

G. Day seven   _____ Creatures that move in the water

                    _____ Cattle

                    _____ Dry land

                    _____ Heaven

                    _____ Oceans

                    _____ Stars

14. How was the earth first described? _____

_____

15. God told Adam and Eve to be _____ and

_____ .

16. Adam and Eve were to have dominion over the _____ ,

_____ , and _____ .

Key Word

To find the key word, fill in the blanks in words 1 through 10 with the missing letters. Transfer those letters to the corresponding numbered squares in the diagram.

1	2	3	4	5	6	7	8	9	10

1. A D A __

2. D __ A D

3. B A __ H

4. __ O L Y

5. F __ R N A C E

6. J A M E __

7. __ V E

8. C A N D __ E

9. __ B S A L O M

10. S __ E E P

Escape To Noah's Ark

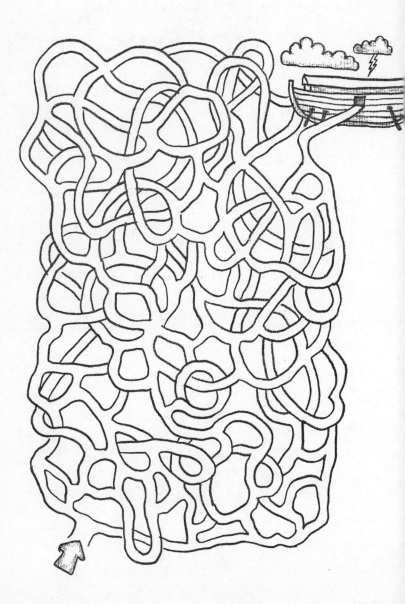

Guess Who

1. Who was the first murderer? _____
2. Who was the oldest man in the Bible? _____
3. Who was called "a friend of God"? _____
4. Who was called "a man after God's own heart"? _____
5. Whose wife was turned into a pillar of salt? _____
6. Who worked seven years to get his wife? _____
7. Who sold his birthright? _____
8. Who had a coat of many colors? _____
9. Who struck a rock? _____
10. Who was swallowed by an earthquake? _____
11. Who held up the arms of Moses? _____
12. Who had a donkey speak to him? _____
13. Who led Israel into the promised land? _____
14. Who were the reliable spies? _____
15. Whose sin brought a defeat in battle? _____
16. Who was the first judge of Israel? _____
17. Who won a battle with 300 men? _____
18. Who was called the "supplanter"? _____
19. Who was a physician in the New Testament? _____

Who Is the Son?

In four moves see if you can discover who was the son of Lamech.

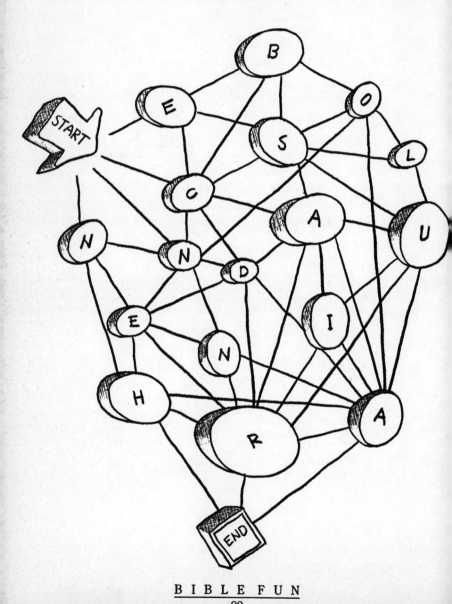

Answers

Answers

Page 7

Beatitudes

1. Poor in spirit
2. Mourn
3. Meek
4. Hunger and thirst after righteousness
5. Merciful, mercy
6. Pure in heart
7. Peacemakers
8. Are persecuted for righteousness sake
9. Revile, persecute, all manner of evil, falsely

Answers

Odd
or Even

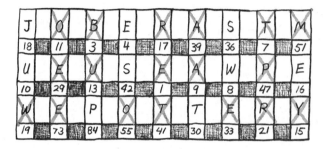

Answers

Answers

Page 10

Something the
Israelites Faced

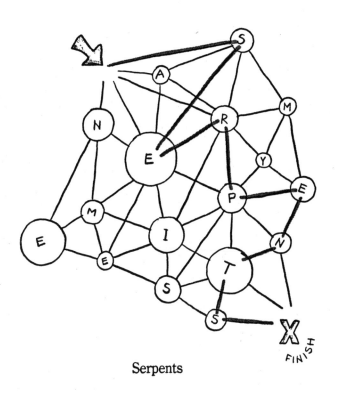

Serpents

Answers

Page 11

Things Missing
In Heaven

1. sea
2. tears
3. death
4. mourning
5. crying
6. pain
7. sun
8. moon
9. insecurity
10. sin
11. night
12. sickness
13. lamps
14. devil
15. hunger
16. thirst
17. heat
18. separation

Answers

Bible
Labyrinth

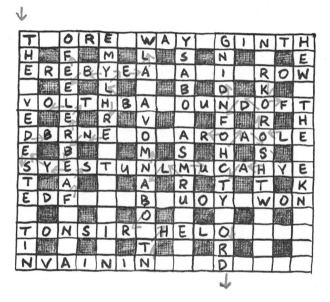

Therefore, my beloved brethren be ye steadfast, unmovable, always abounding in the work of the Lord, for as much as ye know that your labor is not in vain in the Lord.

I Corinthians 15:58

Answers

Mixed
Letters

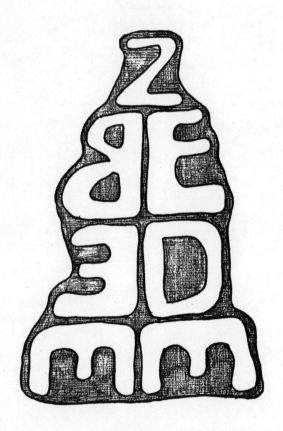

Zebedee

Answers

Descriptions
of Hell

1. Flaming fire — II Thessalonians 1:7,8
2. This flame — Luke 16:24
3. Unquenchable fire — Mark 9:42-48
4. Everlasting fire — Matthew 18:8, 25:41
5. Hell fire — Matthew 5:22, 18:9
6. Furnace of fire — Matthew 13:42, 50
7. Lake of fire — Revelation 19:20, 20:10
9. Shame and everlasting contempt — Daniel 12:2
10. A place of destruction — Philippians 3:19, Matthew 7:13
11. A place of weeping and gnashing of teeth — Matthew 13:42,50
12. Eternal punishment — Matthew 25:46
13. Outer darkness — Matthew 8:12, 22:13
14. The wrath to come — Luke 3:7, Romans 5:9
15. A place of torments — Luke 16:28, Revelation 14:10,11
16. Eternal destruction — II Thessalonians 1:9
17. A place of damnation or condemnation — II Peter 2:3, Jude 4
18. A place of retribution — II Corinthians 11:15, II Thessalonians 1:6
19. The second death — Revelation 20:14, 21:8

Answers

Page 15

Resist
The Devil

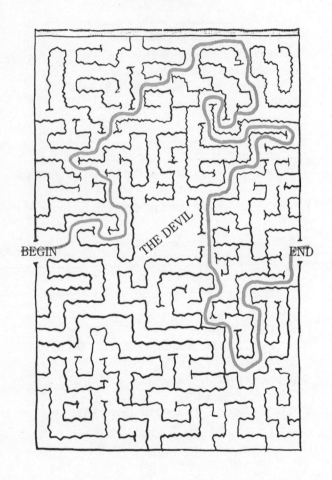

Answers

Page 16
Name
The Event

Gideon defeats the Midianites.
While Gideon's men were blowing their trumpets the
Lord made the enemy troops attack each other.

Judges 7:22

Page 17
Key Word

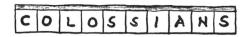

C O L O S S I A N S

Answers

Put Them
In Order

1. Matthew
2. Mark
3. Luke
4. John
5. Acts
6. Romans
7. I Corinthians
8. II Corinthians
9. Galatians
10. Ephesians
11. Philippians
12. Colossians
13. I Thessalonians
14. II Thessalonians
15. I Timothy
16. II Timothy
17. Titus
18. Philemon
19. Hebrews
20. James
21. I Peter
22. II Peter
23. I John
24. II John
25. III John
26. Jude
27. Revelation

Answers

Cain And Abel
And the Old Men

1. Tiller of the ground
2. Keeper of the sheep
3. Cain
4. That he didn't know where his brother was
5. Nod
6. Enoch
7. Jubal
8. Tubal = Cain
9. Methuselah
10. 969 years old
11.
A. Adam	C	905	F. Jared	H	969
B. Seth	E	895	G. Enoch	B	912
C. Enos	G	365	H. Methuselah	I	777
D. Cainan	A	930	I. Lamech	F	962
E. Mahalaleel	D	910			

12. Eight
13. God
14. B. Ararat
15. An olive leaf
16. One year and ten days
17. Be fruitful and multiply
18. Built an altar and thanked God
19. A rainbow
20. Noah

Answers

Patchword

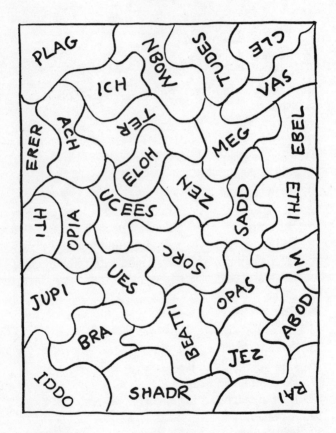

1. Ichabod
2. Plagues
3. Vashti
4. Ethiopia
5. Rainbow
6. Beatitudes
7. Elohim
8. Sadducees
9. Shadrach
10. Cleopas
11. Jezebel
12. Sorcerer
13. Brazen
14. Megiddo
15. Jupiter

Answers

Guess Who

1. Eutychus
2. Elisha
3. Isaiah
4. Lydia
5. Apollos
6. Tyrannus
7. Demetrius
8. Paul and Silas
9. Solomon
10. Jehoshaphat
11. Sanballat
12. Mordecai
13. Haman
14. Eliphaz, Bildad and Zophar
15. Asaph
16. Isaiah
17. Ezekiel
18. Daniel
19. Hosea
20. Jonah

Answers

Choose-a-Letter

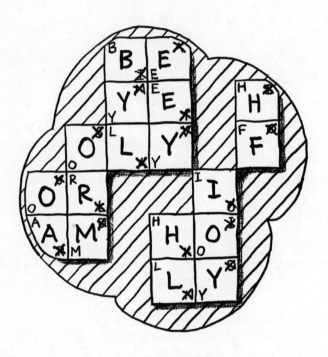

Be ye holy; for I am holy.

I Peter 1:16

Answers

Old Testament
Books

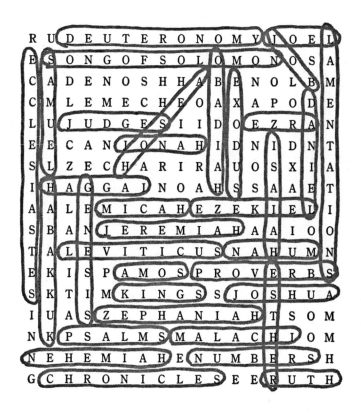

Answers

Skeleton
Fill-in

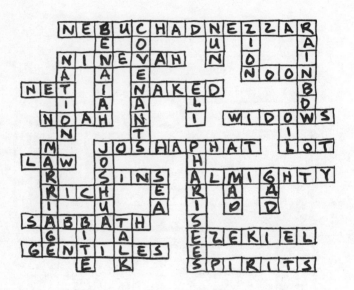

Answers

Choose-a-Letter

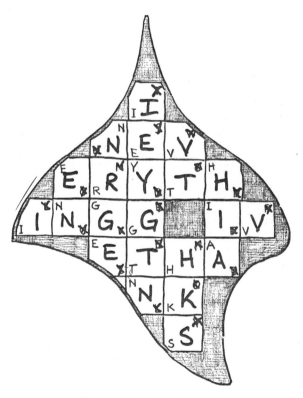

In everything give thanks.

I Thessalonians 5:18

Answers

Doctrinal Studies

1. The study of God — Theology (C)
2. The study of the Bible — Bibliology (D)
3. The study of Christ — Christology (E)
4. The study of angels — Angelology (A)
5. The study of salvation — Soteriology (H)
6. The study of the church — Ecclesiology (B)
7. The study of end-time events — Eschatology (I)
8. The study of the Holy Spirit — Pneumatology (J)
9. The study of man — Anthropology (K)
10. The study of demons — Demonology (F)
11. The study of the descent of families —
    Genealogy (G)

Answers

Tail Tag

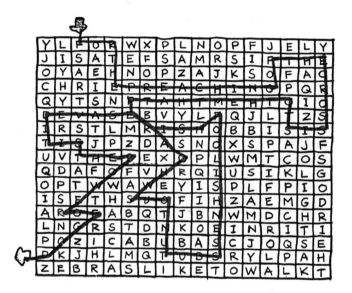

For the preaching of the cross is to them that perish foolishness but unto us who are saved it is the power of God.

I Corinthians 1:18

Answers

Page 29

Jumbles

SCRAMBLED NAME   UNSCRAMBLED NAME

1. M J A E S   (J) A (M) E S
    A N R B A B A S   (B) A R (N) A B A S
    S R I A L E   (I) S R (A) (E) L
    M I N O R D   (N) I M R O D

New scrambled name (J) (M) (B) (N) (I) (A) (E) (N)

Unscrambled name   B E N J A M I N

2. Y R C U S   C Y (R) U S
    M A H   (H) (A) M
    A O J N H   J (O) N (A) (H)
    U A L P   (P) A U L

New scrambled name (R) (H) (A) (O) (A) (H) (P)

Unscrambled name   P H A R A O H

B I B L E F U N

114

Answers

Page 30

A Quote
From Gideon

Show me a sign.

Judges 6:17

Page 31

The Attributes
Of God

1. God is holy
2. God is righteous
3. God is full of grace
4. God is good
5. God is merciful
6. God is a deliverer
7. God is benevolent
8. God is life
9. God is eternal
10. God is a spirit
11. God is full of wisdom
12. God is sovereign
13. God is immense
14. God is self-existent
15. God is a trinity
16. God is a unity
17. God is gentle
18. God is life
19. God is the sustainer
20. God is truth
21. God is just
22. God is long-suffering
23. God is kind
24. God is forgiving
25. God is faithful
26. God is omnipresent (all around)
27. God is personal
28. God is immutable (does not change)
29. God is infinite
30. God is omniscient (all knowing)
31. God foreknows
32. God is omnipotent (all powerful)
33. God is creator
34. God is full of wrath (toward sin)
35. God is jealous (of His holiness)
36. God is light

Answers

Page 32
Name
The Event

Nehemiah rebuilding the wall of Jerusalem
Even those who carried building materials worked with
one hand and kept a weapon in the other.

Nehemiah 4:17

Page 33
Quotation
Puzzle

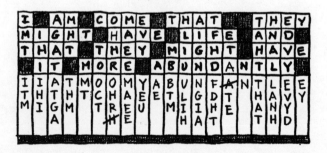

John 10:10

Answers

Versigram

1. And thou shalt love the Lord thy God with all thine heart, and with all thy soul, and with all thy might. Deuteronomy 6:5
2. For other foundation can no man lay than that is laid, which is Jesus Christ. I Corinthians 3:11
3. God is our refuge and strength, a very present help in trouble. Psalms 46:1
4. As ye have therefore received Christ Jesus the Lord, so walk ye in him: rooted and built up in him, and stablished in the faith, as ye have been taught, abounding therein with thanksgiving. Colossians 2:6,7
5. The statutes of the Lord are right, rejoicing the heart: the commandment of the Lord is pure, enlightening the eyes. Psalm 19:8

Answers

Temptation And
Fall of Man

1. Serpent
2. Serpent, surely die
3. Serpent
   E. Become as gods
4. Their eyes were opened and they knew they were naked
5. Sewed fig leaves together and made aprons
6. They hid themselves
   Amongst the trees
7. B. Where art thou?
8. The serpent
9. Eve
10. B. Made him crawl on his belly
11. C. After the fall
12. True
13. True
14. Coats of skins
15. Sent them out of the Garden of Eden
16. Because cherubims (angels) guarded the entrance with a flaming sword
17. Cain
18. Abel

Answers

Name
The Event

Shadrach, Meshach, and Abednego in the fiery furnace
". . . the fourth looks like a son of the gods."

Daniel 3:25 (NIV)

Answers

Alphagram

```
      S N O W
          N O A H
        J O B
          R O M A N
    S T E P H E N
    A H A Z
          M A R T Y R
      P R I N C E
  C H E R U B
      G R E E K
          J U D E
      D E V O T E D
    A L E X A N D E R
A Q U I L A
          S O D O M
E A R T H Q U A K E
          D O V E
        O B A D I A H
    E L E C T V
        C Y R U S
          K I S S
          G I D E O N
      T I T U S
    P S A L M S
    P E R F E C T
          H E A R T
```

Answers

Page 40
Key Word

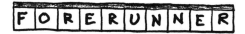

FORERUNNER

Page 41
Escape From
The Circle of Sin

SIN

Answers

Put Them
In Order

1. Genesis
2. Exodus
3. Leviticus
4. Numbers
5. Deuteronomy
6. Joshua
7. Judges
8. Ruth
9. I Samuel
10. II Samuel
11. I Kings
12. II Kings
13. I Chronicles
14. II Chronicles
15. Ezra
16. Nehemiah
17. Esther
18. Job
19. Psalms
20. Proverbs
21. Ecclesiastes
22. Song of Solomon
23. Isaiah
24. Jeremiah
25. Lamentations
26. Ezekiel
27. Daniel
28. Hosea
29. Joel
30. Amos
31. Obadiah
32. Jonah
33. Micah
34. Nahum
35. Habakkuk
36. Zephaniah
37. Haggai
38. Zechariah
39. Malachi

Answers

Abraham

1. Abram
2. Sarai
3. Lot
4. D.   Melchizedek
5. Hagar
6. Ishmael
7. 100
8. B.   A ram
9. C.   6 times
10. A friend of God
11. Laughed
12. 0, 2
13. Fire, Brimstone
14. She turned into a pillar of salt
15. False
16. A great nation
17. 127
18. 2
19. D.   A half sister
20. D.   175

Answers

Page 45

Names and Titles
of Jesus

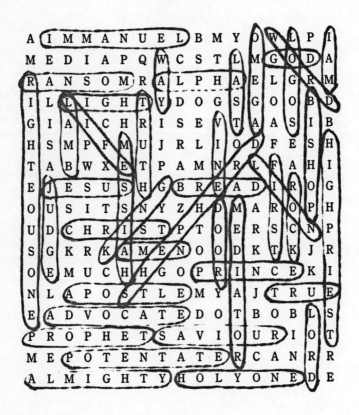

Answers

Name
The Event

Solomon judges a difficult case

"Cut the living child in two and give half to one and half to the other."

I Kings 3:25 (NIV)

Answers

A Place
For Every One

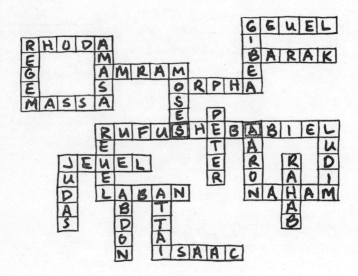

Answers

Gifts of
the Spirit

1. Word of wisdom
2. Word of knowledge
3. Faith
4. Healing
5. Miracles
6. Prophecy
7. Discerning of spirits
8. Tongues
9. Interpretation of tongues
10. Ministry
11. Teaching
12. Exhortation
13. Giving
14. Administration
15. Mercy

Answers

Bible
Labyrinth

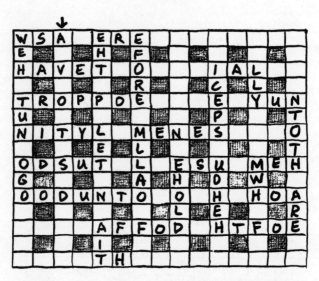

As we have therefore opportunity, let us do good unto all men, especially unto them who are of the household of faith.

Galatians 6:10

Answers

Jumbles

SCRAMBLED NAME   UNSCRAMBLED NAME

1. G A G A   A (G) A G
   S U P P I H C R A   (A) R C H I (P) (P) U S
   N N A A S I A   A N A N (I) A S
   B N A R E   (A) B N E (R)

   New scrambled name   (G) (A) (P) (P) (I) (A) (R)
   Unscrambled name   A   G   R   I   P   P   A

2. Q U A A L I   (A) Q U I L (A)
   M O S A   A (M) O S
   Z O R A   (A) Z O (R)
   K B K A H A U K   (H) A (B) A K K U K

   New scrambled name   (A) (A) (M) (A) (R) (H) (B)
   Unscrambled name   A   B   R   A   H   A   M

Key Word

Answers

Patchword

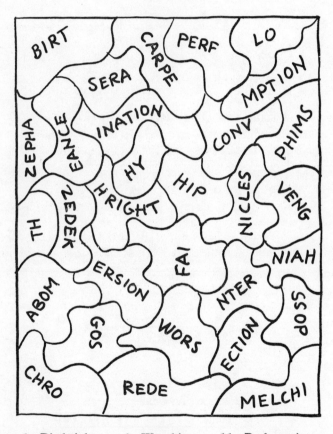

1. Birthright
2. Logos
3. Seraphims
4. Chronicles
5. Melchizedek
6. Worship
7. Carpenter
8. Perfection
9. Zephaniah
10. Faith
11. Redemption
12. Abomination
13. Hyssop
14. Vengeance
15. Conversion

Answers

Alphanumber

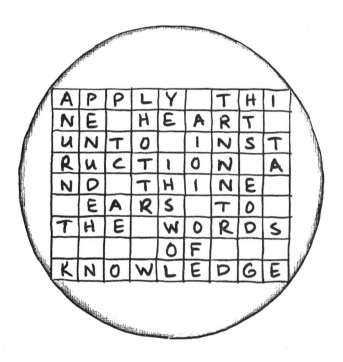

Proverbs 23:12

Answers

Noah And
The Flood

1. 120
2. Grace
3. Shem, Ham, Japeth
4. B. Gopher
5. Pitch
6. 300, 50, 30
7. 1
8. 3
9. Two of every kind except for seven of each kind of the clean animals and birds
10. Forty
11. E. 600
12. Eight
13. The Lord
14. B. Ararat
15. An olive leaf
16. One year and ten days
17. Be fruitful and multiply
18. Built an altar and offered burnt offerings
19. A rainbow
20. Noah

Answers

Page 56

The Escape From
Darkness to Light

Answers

Famous People
Match

1. Ishmael — Archer (K)
2. Nimrod — Mighty hunter (Q)
3. Esau — Cunning hunter (E)
4. Paul — Tentmaker (L)
5. Peter — Fisherman (C)
6. Matthew — Tax collector (P)
7. Saul — King (M)
8. David — Giant killer (O)
9. Simon — Magician (N)
10. Esther — Queen (H)
11. Deborah — Judge (B)
12. Anna — Prophetess (A)
13. Gabriel — Angel (F)
14. Nicodemus — Pharisee (G)
15. Nehemiah — Wall builder (J)
16. Aaron — High priest (I)
17. Lydia — Purple cloth seller (S)
18. Pilate — Governor (T)
19. Micah — Prophet (R)
20. Samson — Slayer with jaw bone (D)

Answers

A Quote
From Ruth

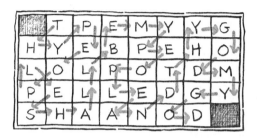

Thy people shall be my people and thy God my God.

Ruth 1:16

Name
The Event

Cain and Abel bringing offerings to the Lord "Why are you angry? Why is your face downcast?"

Genesis 4:6 (NIV)

Answers

Odd
Or Even

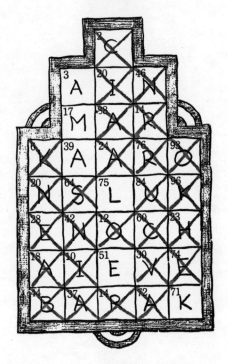

Amalek

Joseph

1. H. Benjamin
2. J. Something Joseph rode
3. L. Silver cup
4. G. Wept aloud
5. C. The name Pharoah gave Joseph
6. I. An abomination to the Egyptians
7. K. The field of Machpelah
8. A. A dream of Pharoah
9. E. Beersheba
10. B. The wife Pharoah gave J
11. D. Goshen
12. F. The sons of Joseph

Answers

Mixed
Letters

John the Baptist

Clusters

1. Jerusha, Abigail, Leah, Herodias, Sarah, Cornelia, Dinah
2. Eunice, Eve, Damaris, Sapphira, Anna, Bilhah, Dorcas, Salome
3. Orpah, Zilpah, Abishag, Dursilla, Vashti, Jezebel, Mary
4. Gomer, Rachel, Lydia, Bernice, Esther, Ruth, Tamar, Rhoda

Answers

Page 64

Help Paul
and Silas Escape

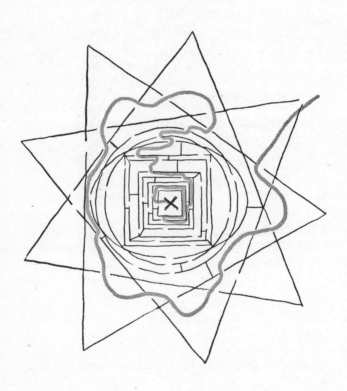

Answers

Things
God Hates

1. A proud look
2. A lying tongue
3. Hands that shed innocent blood
4. A heart that deviseth wicked imaginations
5. Feet swift in running to mischief
6. A false witness that speaketh lies
7. He that soweth discord among the brethren

Answers

Page 66

Bible
Labyrinth

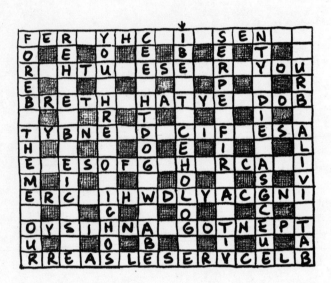

I beseech you therefore brethren by the mercies of God that ye present your bodies a living sacrifice, holy, acceptable unto, God which is your reasonable service.

Romans 12:1

Answers

Page 67

A Quote
From Adam

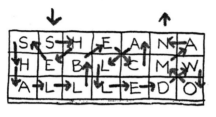

She shall be
called woman.

Genesis 2:23

Page 68

Anticipation

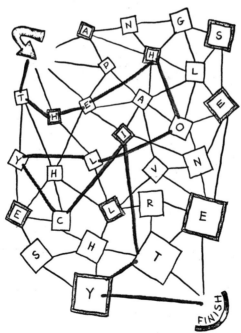

The Holy City

Answers

Page 69

A Place For
Every One

Answers

Ten
Commandments

1. Thou shalt have no other gods before me.
2. Thou shalt not make unto thee any graven image.
3. Thou shalt not take the name of the Lord thy God in vain.
4. Remember the sabbath day to keep it holy.
5. Honor thy father and mother.
6. Thou shalt not kill.
7. Thou shalt not commit adultery.
8. Thou shalt not steal.
9. Thou shalt not bear false witness.
10. Thou shalt not covet.

Exodus 20:3-17

Answers

David's
Scroll

The Lord is my shepherd;
I shall not want.
He maketh me to lie down in green pastures:
he leadeth me beside the still waters.
He restoreth my soul:
he leadeth me in the paths of righteousness for his
name's sake.
Yea, though I walk through the valley of the shadow of
death,
I will fear no evil:
for thou art with me;
thy rod and thy staff they comfort me.
Thou preparest a table before me in the presence of
mine enemies:
thou anointest my head with oil;
my cup runneth over.
Surely goodness and mercy shall follow me
all the days of my life:
and I will dwell in the house of the Lord forever.

Answers

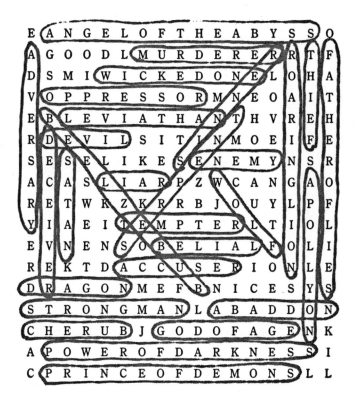

Page 72

Names and Designations For Satan

```
E A N G E L O F T H E A B Y S S O
A G O O D L M U R D E R E R R T F
D S M I W I C K E D O N E L O H A
V O P P R E S S O R M N E O A I T
E B L E V I A T H A N T H V R E H
R D E V I L S I T I N M O E I F E
S E S E L I K E S E N E M Y N S R
A C A S L I A R P Z W C A N G A O
R E T W K Z K R R B J O U Y L P F
Y I A E I T E M P T E R L T I O L
E V N E N S O B E L I A L F O L I
R E K T D A C C U S E R I O N L E
D R A G O N M E F B N I C E S Y S
S T R O N G M A N L A B A D D O N
C H E R U B J G O D O F A G E N K
A P O W E R O F D A R K N E S S I
C P R I N C E O F D E M O N S L L
```

Answers

Page 73

Name
The Event

Feeding of the five thousand.
"We have here only five loaves of bread and two fish."

Matthew 14:17 (NIV)

Page 74

Help Jonah
Escape

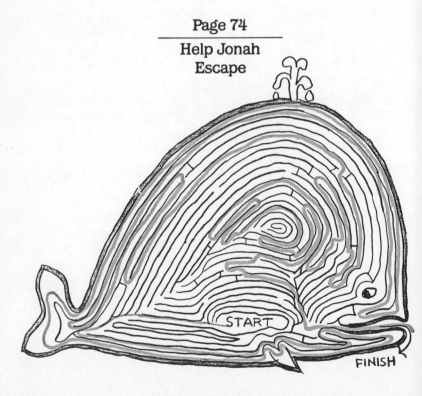

Answers

Page 75,76

Adam
and Eve

1. D. Dust
2. Breathed in his nostrils the breath of life
3. Eden
4. Tree of life, Tree of knowledge of good and evil
5. A river
6. 1. Pison
   2. Gihon
   3. Hiddekel
   4. Euphrates
7. To dress and keep the garden
8. C. Die
9. Adam
10. Out of one of Adam's ribs
11. Woman
12. It is not good for man to be alone

Answers

Page 77
Name
The Event

Isaac blesses Jacob.
"So he went to him and kissed him. When Isaac caught
the smell of his clothes, he blessed him . . ."

Genesis 27:27

Page 78
Alphanumber

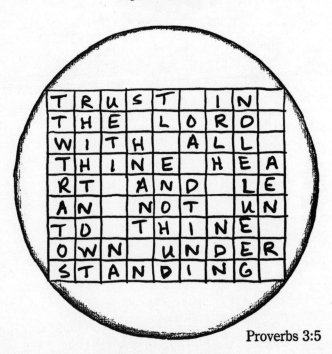

T	R	U	S	T		I	N
T	H	E		L	O	R	D
W	I	T	H		A	L	L
T	H	I	N	E		H	E	A
R	T		A	N	D		L	E
A	N		N	O	T		U	N
T	O		T	H	I	N	E
O	W	N		U	N	D	E	R
S	T	A	N	D	I	N	G

Proverbs 3:5

Answers

Page 79

The Circle
of Love

- How many circles are there in the puzzle?   47
- How many times is the letter "L" used?   28
- How many times is the letter "O" used?   31
- How many times is the letter "V" used?   33
- How many times is the letter "E" used?   42
- How many small circles contain the letter "L"?   48
- How many small circles contain the letter "O"?   63
- How many small circles contain the letter "V"?   72
- How many small circles contain the letter "E"?   85

Page 80

Joseph

1. False
2. True
3. False
4. True
5. Colors
6. Reuben
7. Midianite, 20
8. An evil beast
9. Potiphar
10. Butler, Baker
11. The chief butler

Answers

Page 81

Odd
or Even

Rejoice evermore.

Page 82

Houses for
the Scholar

1. Bethbarah (H)
2. Bethany (I)
3. Betharabah (J)
4. Bethaven (K)
5. Bethphage (L)
6. Bethbiri (R)
7. Bethcar (B)
8. Bethdiblathaim (S)
9. Bethel (T)
10. Bethemek (A)
11. Bethesda (D)
12. Bethgader (C)
13. Bethgamul (E)
14. Bethaccerem (F)
15. Bethharan (G)
16. Bethhogla (M)
17. Bethleaphrah (N)
18. Bethlebaoth (O)
19. Bethlehem (P)
20. Bethsaida (Q)

Answers

1. Adam—a type of Christ (D)
2. Amalek—a type of the flesh (E)
3. Ark—a type of salvation (F)
4. Blue—a type of Heaven (G)
5. Brass—a type of righteous judgment (B)
6. Candlestick—a type of the Holy Spirit (A)
7. Rock—a type of Christ (D)
8. Lamb—a type of Christ (D)
9. Fig leaves—a type of human righteousness (K)
10. Fire—a type of judgment (H)
11. Horn—a type of power, strength and honor (O)
12. Leprosy—a type of sin (C)
13. Leaven—a type of evil teaching (I)
14. Lion—a type of strength and power (J)
15. Oil—a type of the Holy Spirit (A)
16. Rainbow—a type of grace and mercy (L)
17. Wine—a type of joy (M)
18. Hammer—a type of the Word of God (N)
19. Water—a type of the Word of God (N)
20. Sword—a type of the Word of God (N)

Answers

Skeleton
Fill-in

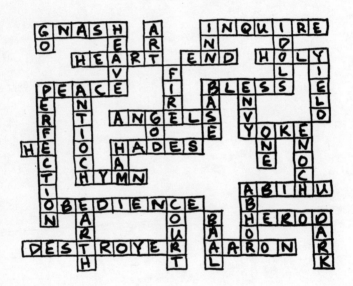

Answers

Seals, Trumpets And Vials

1. Q—Death
2. R—Fourth trumpet
3. M—Famine
4. P—Third vial
5. O—First trumpet
6. B—Sixth trumpet
7. J—First vial
8. C—War
9. F—Fifth vial
10. A—Second trumpet

11. L—Fifth trumpet
12. T—Destruction
13. D—Seventh trumpet
14. K—Sixth vial
15. G—Conquering horse and rider
16. E—Second vial
17. H—Third trumpet
18. S—Fourth vial
19. N—Seventh vial
20. I—Persecution

Answers

Clusters

1. Zillah, Candace, Priscilla, Naomi, Phoebe, Joanna
2. Hagar, Zipporah, Martha, Jochebed, Delilah, Keturah
3. Sapphira, Miriam, Michal, Lois, Susanna, Elisabeth, Chloe
4. Claudia, Rahab, Bathsheba, Judith, Deborah, Phoebe, Rebekah

Answers

Creation

1. Heaven, earth
2. C. "Let there be light."
3. True
4. Heaven
5. Spirit of God
6. Earth
7. Seas
8. B. third
9. Fifth day
10. False
11. That it was good
12. Rested
13. F Creeping things
    A Light
    E Winged fowl
    C Tree yielding fruit
    F Man
    G Nothing
    E Creatures that move in the water
    F Cattle
    C Dry land
    B Heaven
    C Oceans
    D Stars
14. Without form and void
15. Fruitful, multiply
16. Fish, the fowl, everything that creeps

Answers

Page 89

Key
Word

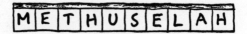

Answers

Escape To Noah's Ark

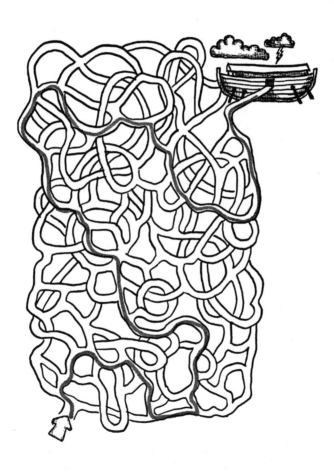

Answers

Guess
Who

1. Cain
2. Methuselah
3. Abraham
4. David
5. Lot
6. Jacob
7. Esau
8. Joseph
9. Moses
10. Korah

11. Aaron and Hur
12. Balaam
13. Joshua
14. Joshua and Caleb
15. Achan
16. Othniel
17. Gideon
18. Jacob
19. Luke

Answers

Who Is
the Son?

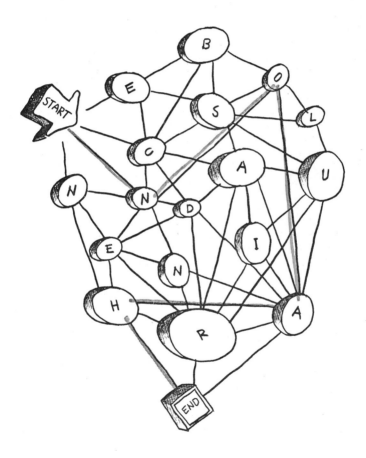

Noah

Other Books by Bob Phillips

- *World's Greatest Collection of Clean Jokes*
- *More Good Clean Jokes*
- *The Last of the Good Clean Jokes*
- *The Return of the Good Clean Jokes*
- *The All American Joke Book*
- *The World's Greatest Collection of Heavenly Humor*
- *The World's Greatest Collection of Riddles and Daffy Definitions*
- *The World's Greatest Collection of Knock, Knock Jokes and Tongue Twisters*
- *The Best of the Good Clean Jokes*
- *Wit and Wisdom*
- *Humor Is Tremendous*
- *The All New Clean Joke Book*
- *Good Clean Jokes for Kids*
- *The Encyclopedia of Good Clean Jokes*
- *Ultimate Good Clean Jokes for Kids*
- *Wacky Good Clean Jokes for Kids* (coming July 1993)
- *Bible Fun*
- *Heavenly Fun*
- *The Ultimate Bible Trivia Challenge*
- *The Little Book of Bible Trivia*
- *How Can I Be Sure? A Pre-Marriage Inventory*
- *Anger Is a Choice*
- *Redi-Reference*
- *Redi-Reference Daily Bible Reading Plan*
- *The Delicate Art of Dancing with Porcupines*
- *Powerful Thinking for Powerful Living*

- *God's Hand Over Hume*

- *Praise Is a Three-Lettered Word—Joy*

- *The Handbook for Headache Relief*

- *Friendship, Love & Laughter*

For information on how to purchase any of the above books, contact your local bookstore or send a self-addressed stamped envelope to:

Family Services
P.O. Box 9363
Fresno, CA 93702